MID-ELEMENTARY

TAKE A BOW!

8 SPARKLING PIANO SOLOS

GREAT RECITAL PIECES!

BOOK 2

BY CAROLYN MILLER

T0081939

ISBN 978-1-61774-265-1

WILLIS MUSIC

EXCLUSIVELY DISTRIBUTED BY

HAL•LEONARD® CORPORATION

7777 W. BLUEMOUND RD. P.O. BOX 13819 MILWAUKEE, WI 53213

Visit Hal Leonard Online at
www.halleonard.com

FROM THE COMPOSER

Recital time should be a happy time! I believe that the recital solo should be carefully chosen to give each student the best chance for success in front of an unfamiliar audience. It is my hope that students will master the carefully selected solos in this book so that a winning performance takes place.

Like *Book 1*, I have included a variety of pieces. Two of my favorites—"Drifting" and "A Gentle Breeze"—portray peaceful images through soft, rolling arpeggios. Some titles can help with imagination and making the pieces come to life. For example, standing in line at the movies and hearing the sound of "Popcorn" popping! In "Bouncing," think of things that bounce— the first thing that comes to my mind is a basketball, or maybe being on a trampoline. In addition, these two pieces focus especially on technical skills. I love to have my students make up a story to go along with "The Frog." Some students tell me the B section includes a big bullfrog and a little baby frog. That visualization has helped them understand *melody* (big frog) and *accompaniment* (baby frog).

My wish is that these pieces will entertain as well as motivate students of any age.

Please enjoy!

Carolyn Miller

CONTENTS

The Frog

Carolyn Miller

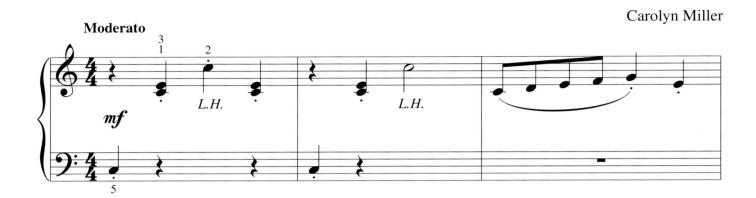

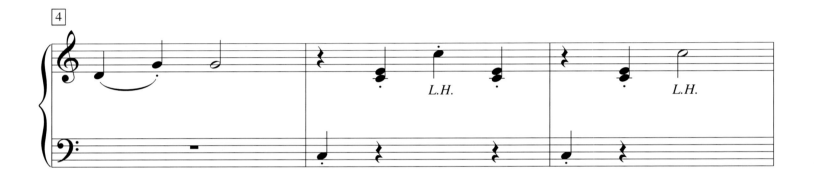

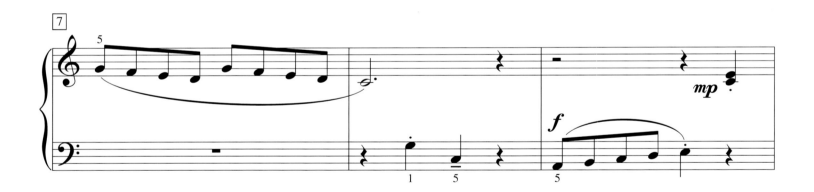

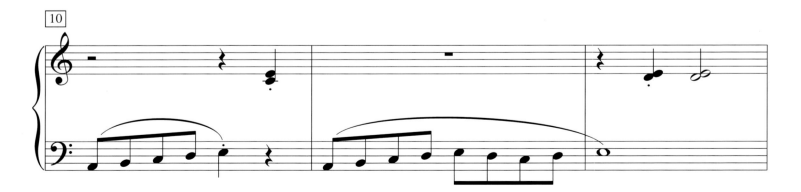

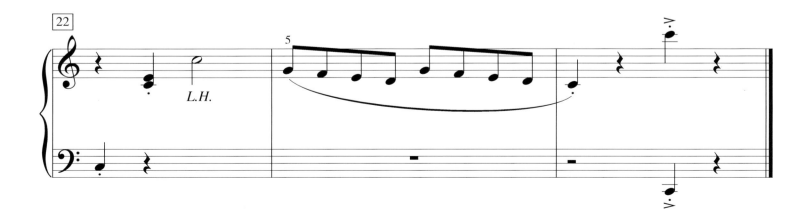

Popcorn

Carolyn Miller

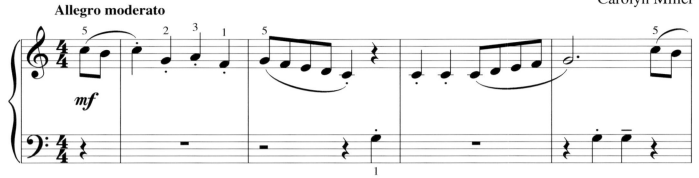

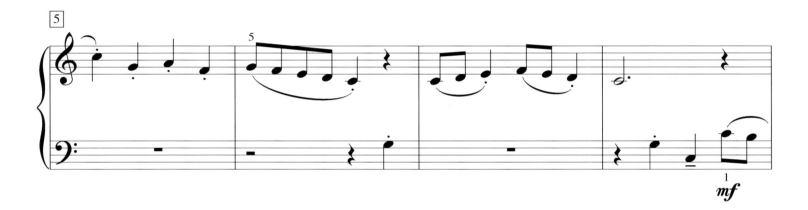

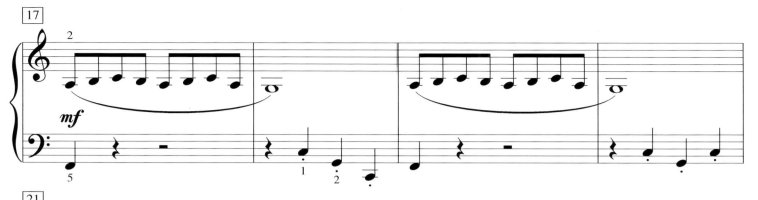

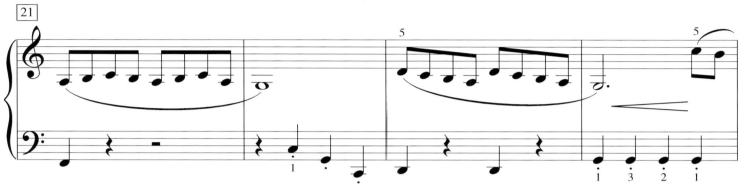

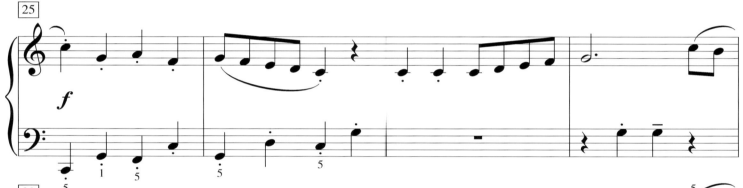

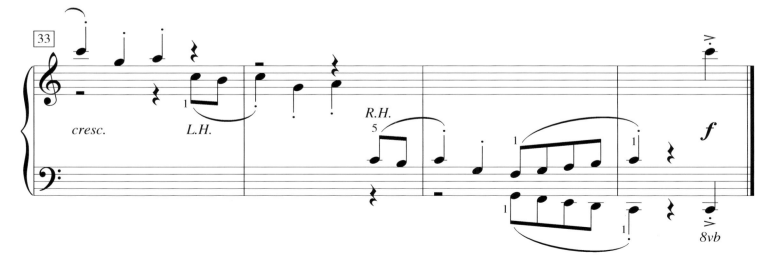

A Little Swing

Carolyn Miller

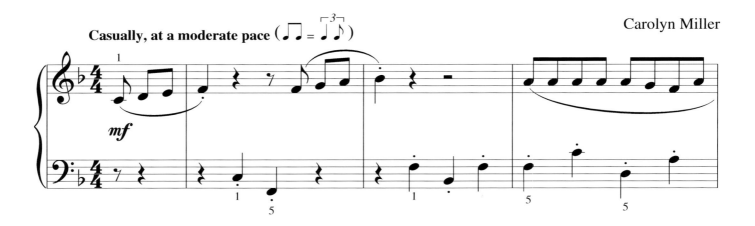

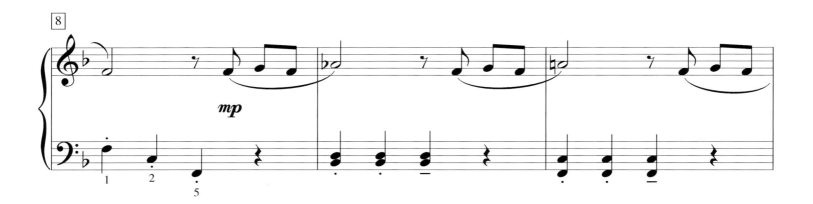

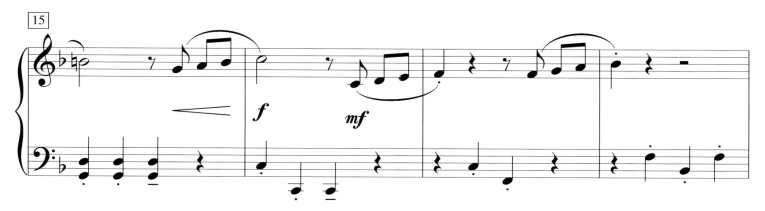

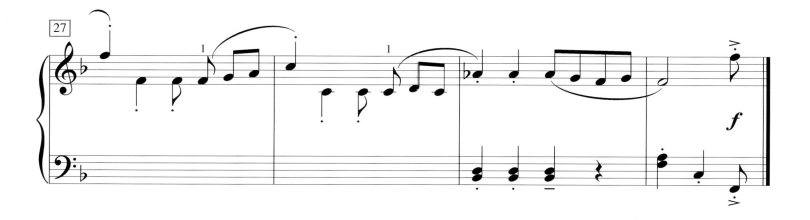

Bouncing

Carolyn Miller

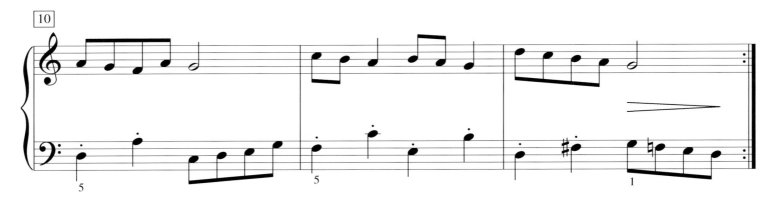

Race to the Finish

Carolyn Miller

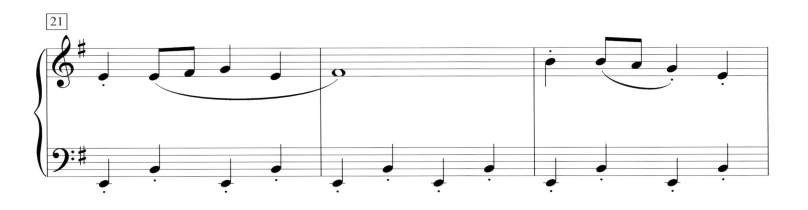

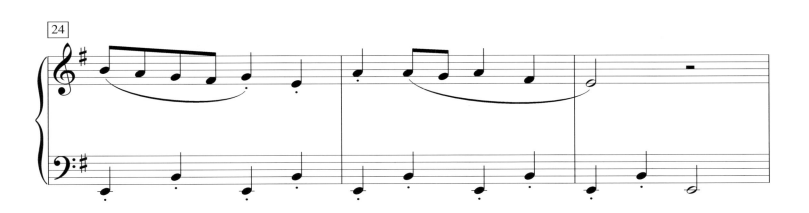

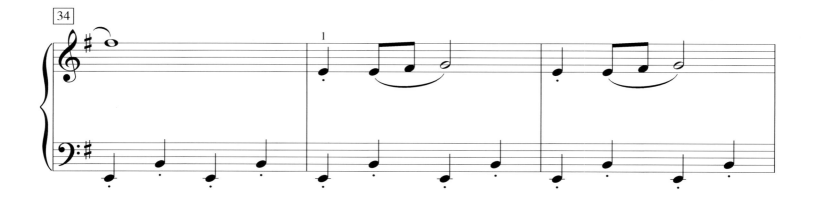

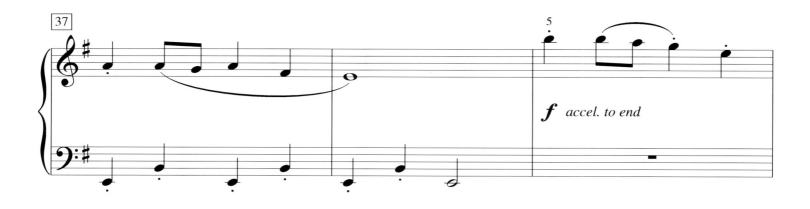

Gorilla in the Wild

Carolyn Miller

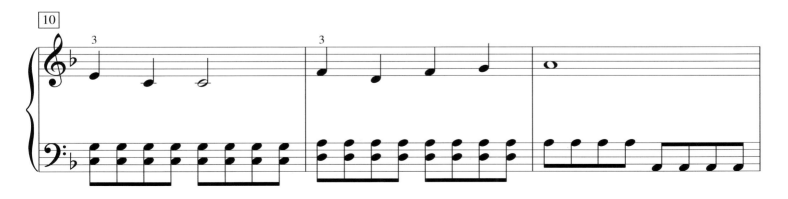

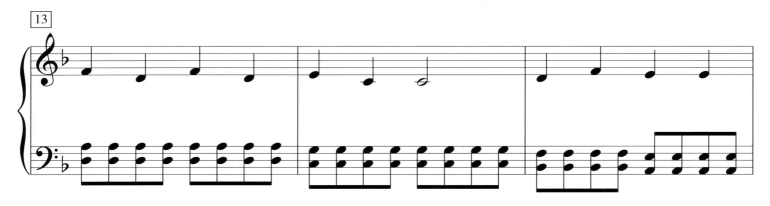

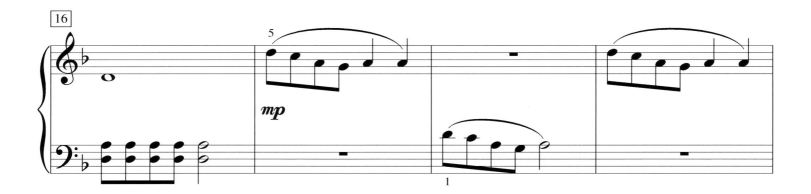

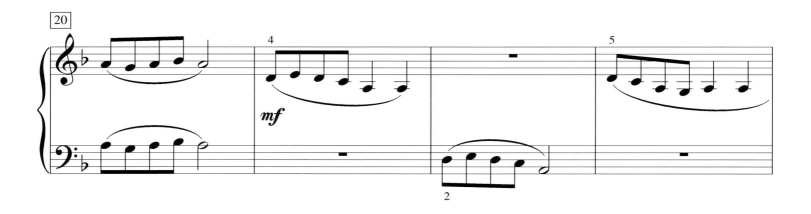

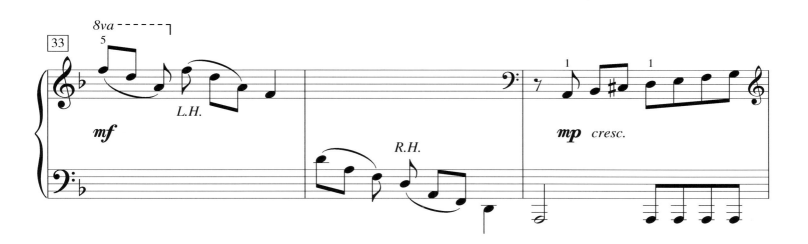

Gentle Breeze

Carolyn Miller

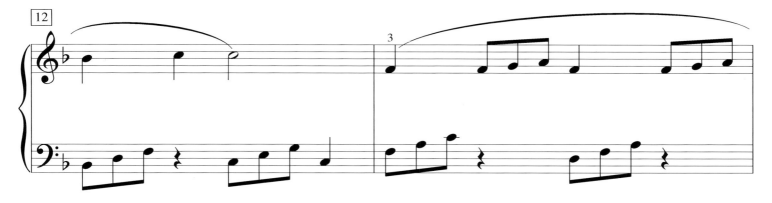

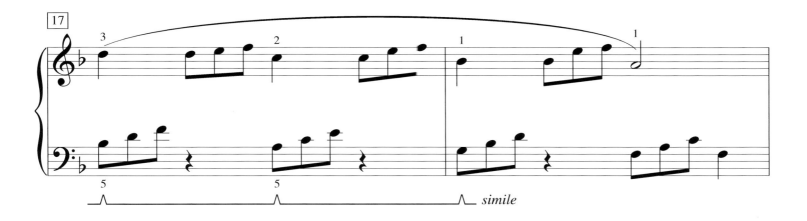

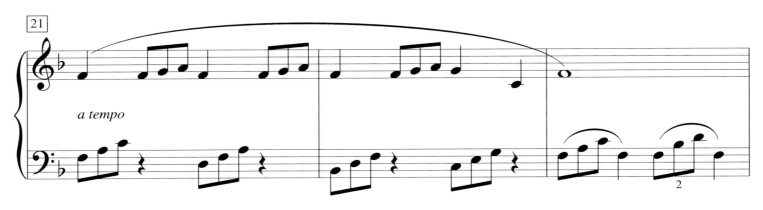

Gently flowing

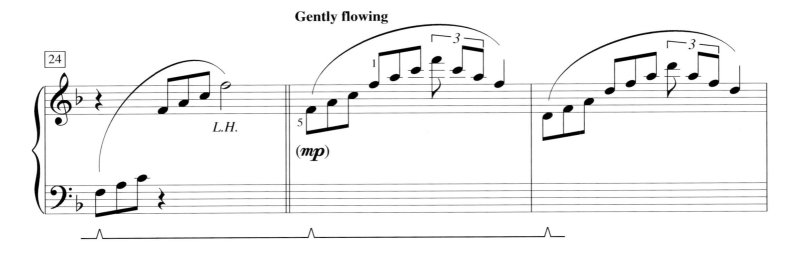

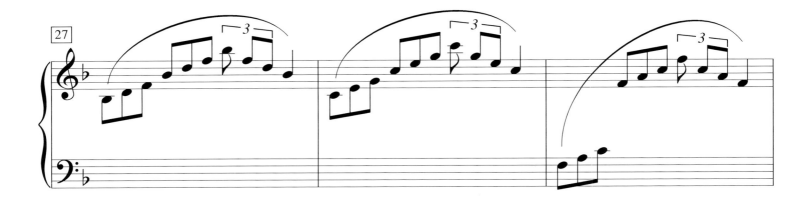

Drifting

Carolyn Miller

With an easy motion (♩ = ca. 132)

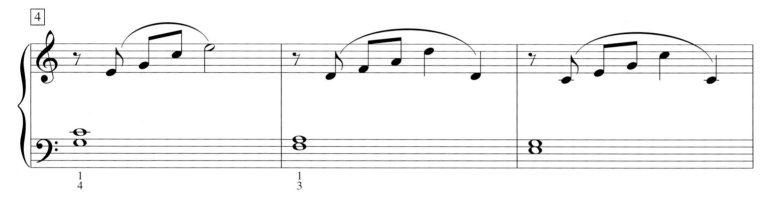

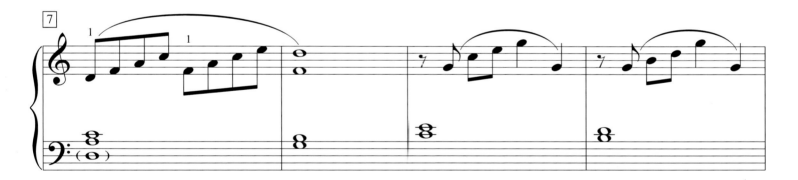

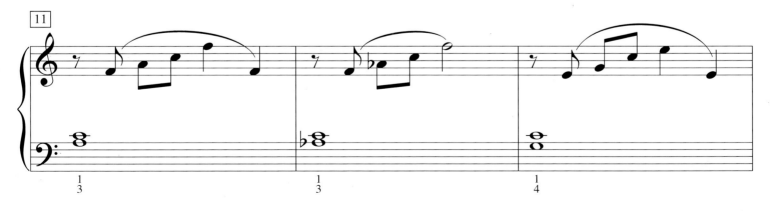

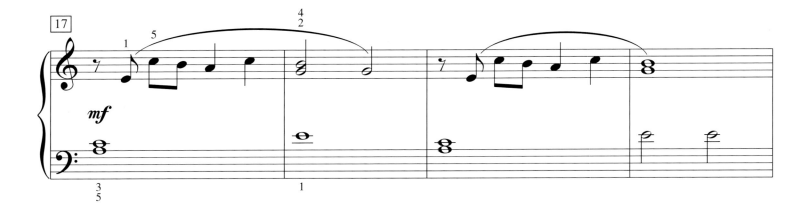

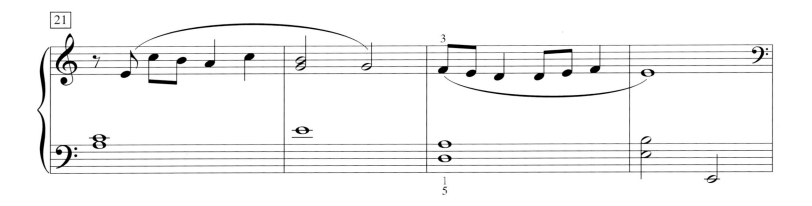

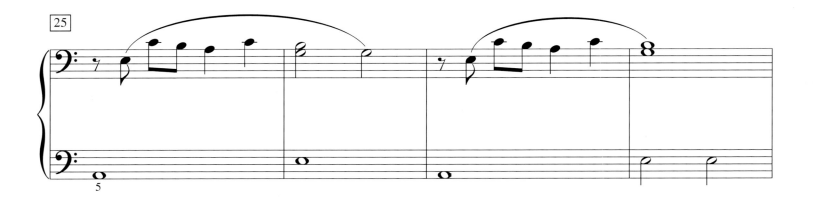

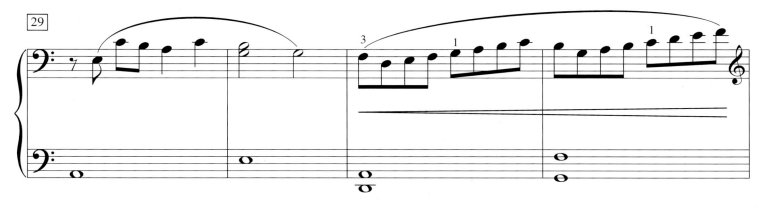

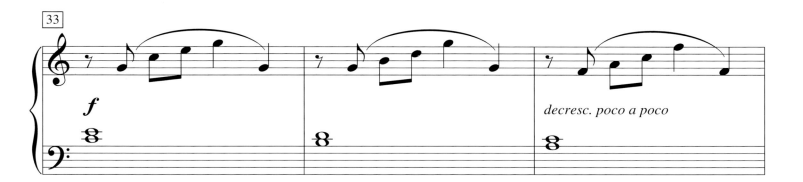

ABOUT THE COMPOSER

Carolyn Miller's teaching and composing career spans over 40 prolific years. She graduated with honors from the College Conservatory of Music at the University of Cincinnati with a degree in music education, and later earned a masters degree in elementary education from Xavier University. Carolyn regularly presents workshops throughout the United States and is a frequent adjudicator at festivals and competitions. Although she recently retired from the Cincinnati public school system, she continues to maintain her own private studio.

Carolyn's music emphasizes essential technical skills. is remarkably fun to play, and appeals to both children and adults. Well-known television personality Regis Philbin performed her pieces "Rolling River" and "Fireflies" in 1992 and 1993 on national television. Carolyn's compositions appear frequently on state contest lists, including the NFMC Festivals Bulletin. She is listed in the *Who's Who in America* and *Who's Who of American Women*.

In her spare time Carolyn directs the Northminster Presbyterian Church Choir in Cincinnati, Ohio and enjoys spending time with her family, especially her seven grandchildren.